Join the Adventure

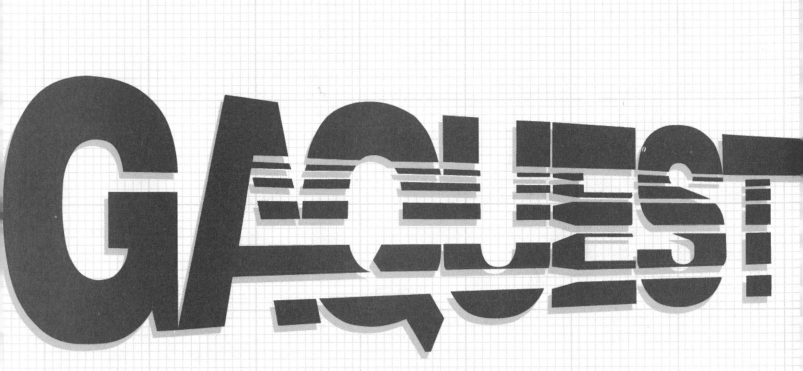

GAMEQUEST

and Learn How to Draw It

BEN GIBSON & SERGE MARCOS

A Perigee Book

500998558

WE WOULD LIKE TO THANK OUR FAMILIES:
DREW, PAULA, AND PATRICK GIBSON AND SERGIO, FE,
AND MARISA MARCOS FOR THEIR LOVE AND SUPPORT.
WE WOULD ALSO LIKE TO THANK OUR PUBLISHER, JOHN DUFF,
AND OUR EDITOR, ADRIENNE SCHULTZ,
FOR THEIR GUIDANCE AND FAITH.

A Perigee Book
Published by The Berkley Publishing Group
A division of Penguin Group (USA) Inc.
375 Hudson Street

Copyright © 2005 Ben Gibson and Serge Marcos
Cover art and design by Ben Gibson and Serge Marcos
Interior art and design by Ben Gibson and Serge Marcos

First Perigee paperback edition: July 2005

Visit our website at
www.penguin.com

Liibrary of Congress Cataloging-in-Publication Data

Giibson, Ben and Marcos, Serge

Manga Quest
Join the Adventure and Learn to Draw It/
Ben Gibson and Serge Marcos.—
1st Perigee ed.
p. cm.
"A Perigee Book."
ISBN 0-399-53159-9
1.Manga. 2. Art Instruction.

Printed in the United States of America
10 9 8 7 6 5 4 3 2 1

Most Perigee Books are available at special quantity discounts for bulk purchases for sales promotions, premiums, fund-raising or educational use. SPecial books, or book excerpts, can also be created to fit specific needs.

For details, write: Special Markets, The Berkley Publishing Group, 375 Hudson Street, New York, New York 10014

Manga is a centuries-old art form spanning the sketchbooks of legendary Japanese masters Hokusai and Hiroshige to present-day practitioners such as Hiroaki Samura and Katsuhiro Otomo and their multivolume tomes. To the casual dilettante manga is just big eyes, voluptuous girls, guns, robots, and motion lines. But to its creators and connoisseurs manga is much more than mere entertainment. To them it captures the human experience in the subtle pacing, masterful draftsmanship, and poetic toning of the page.

Manga is no longer made solely in Japan. Manga artists from countries outside of Asia are also gaining notoriety, and it has grown into a worldwide phenomenon with numerous translations read by millions across the globe. One reason for manga's global appeal is its great breadth of subject matter—from historical epics, sports sagas, and fantastical science fiction, to teenage romance and children's adventures. There is a manga for everyone.

It should be no surprise, then, that the interest to create manga has increased alongside its book sales. What we offer in this book is a brief introduction to the archtypal characters, creatures, devices, and mecha that inhabit the manga universe. No one book can replace the years of training and practice that any serious manga artist requires. But this book can help you bridge the gap from student to professional. And for those of you who enjoy drawing manga simply as an entertaining diversion, you will no doubt pick up many tricks of the trade here to hone your craft with. Don't be afraid to tread off the beaten path of the manga artist and make mistakes, for it is somewhere between these errors and successes where you will learn what makes you and your manga unique. And with that, we leave you with our very own manga quest.

Enjoy,
Ben & Serge

To be continued...by you!

Will Ed and Kumi escape the evil that is chasing them?
Will they ever find Moxie?

Use the tips and tools you learned to decide the fate
of our friends. Invent new characters, draw new worlds,
and begin your own MANGAQUEST.

INTRODUCTION: GETTING STARTED

10

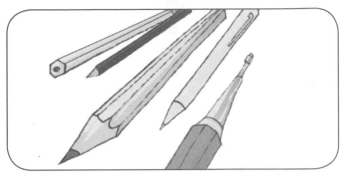

SUPPLIES

PENCILS
Use a good variety of pencils with varying lead consistencies 2H, 2B, HB. Softer leads (ranging from 6b-2b) can be used for darker, expressive lines. Harder leads (6H-2H) are used for underdrawing and in areas where precision line work is critical.

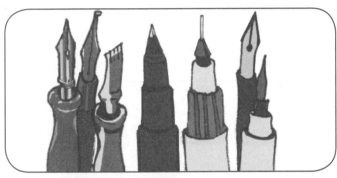

PENS, NIBS, CROQUILS, & MECHANICAL PENS
These are the tools you'll use to ink your pencil drawings for reproduction. Use whatever you're most comfortable with. Brush pens, nibs, and croquils will give you a varied line width and consistency for more emotional expressive drawings. Mechanical and ball point pens will give a more controlled, precise, and uniform line for a clean technical look.

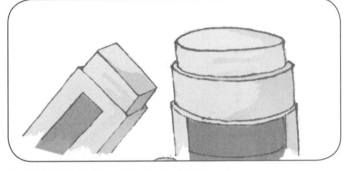

ERASERS & CORRECTION FLUID
For mistakes—no one is perfect! Use white soft erasers for correcting your pencil drawings. For cleaning up ink drawings, use opaque white or correction fluid.

INKS
Water-soluble and waterproof inks should be used to get your pencil drawings ready for reproduction. Sumi ink provides a rich black tone, while Speedball Waterproof is good for water resistance.

RULERS & T-SQUARE
Used for measuring and figuring out design space on a page. They are also used for making straight lines and as a base for triangles.

RAZORS & SHARPENERS
Use these to sharpen your wooden pencils. Which one you use is a matter of personal preference.

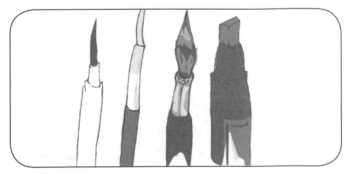

BRUSHES & MARKERS
Used for inking and filling in large areas of black or white. They can also be used to add an even bolder or more expressive line quality to drawings.

TRIANGLES
Use these when drawing angled lines for perspective drawing, cityscapes, vehicles, robots, and other objects.

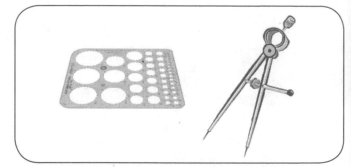

ELLIPSES/CIRCLE TEMPLATES & COMPASS
These are used for drawing round, cylindrical, and spherical objects.

FLEXIBLE CURVE
Use this malleable tool when drawing and/or inking complex curves and arcs.

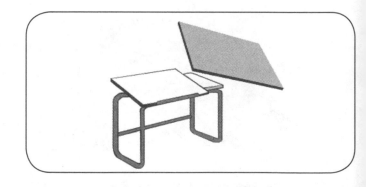

SKETCHBOOK
A nice way of keeping ideas, drawings, and clippings/reference together in a sturdy, portable, bound format.

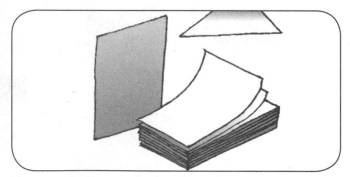

PAPERS
While there are a wide variety of papers available, you should use Bristol board (60-100lb.) for your final, inked illustration. Use inexpensive bond paper (20-40lb) for initial sketches, underdrawings, corrections, and experiments.

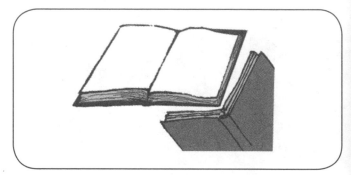

DRAFTING TABLE/DRAWING BOARD
Use these for a surface to lay out your tools and to draw on. A drafting table is designed for in-studio use, while a drawing board is used for on-location sketching.

CHAPTER 1: DRAWING HUMANOIDS

SO WHERE DO WE START?
WELL, JUDGING BY YOUR DRAWINGS YOU NEED TO WORK ON YOUR CHARACTERS.
AND I KNOW THE PERFECT PLACE TO BEGIN.
IT'S THE ONE-STOP SHOP FOR ALL YOUR CHARACTER DESIGN NEEDS.
THE MALL?

The antihero is the bad boy of the manga universe. He lives on the fringe of society and is primarily concerned with his own well-being (and personal fortune).

...NOT SURE IF THIS COSTUME IS THE BEST FIT FOR YOU, ED.

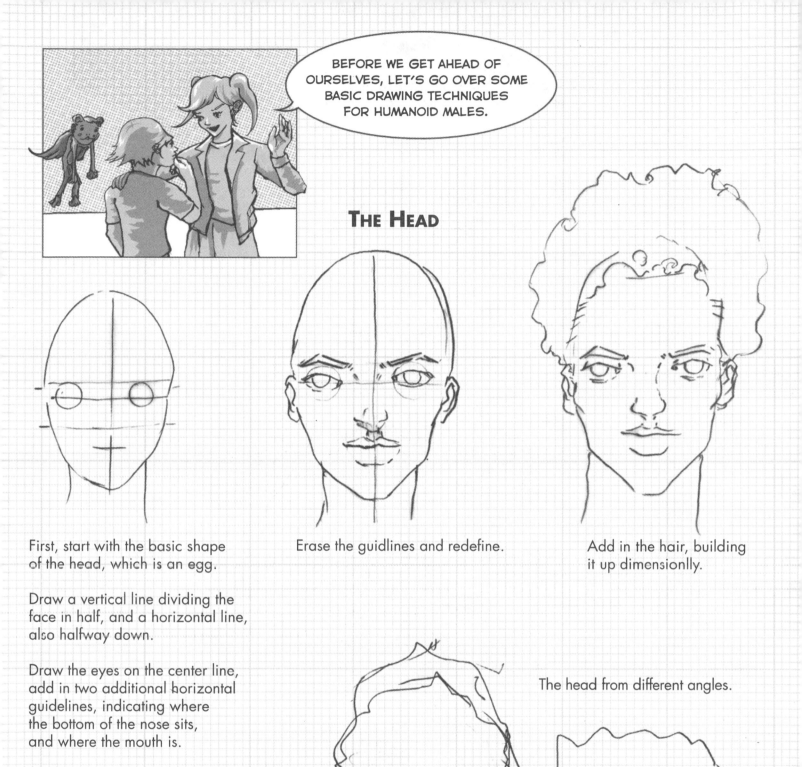

BEFORE WE GET AHEAD OF OURSELVES, LET'S GO OVER SOME BASIC DRAWING TECHNIQUES FOR HUMANOID MALES.

THE HEAD

First, start with the basic shape of the head, which is an egg.

Draw a vertical line dividing the face in half, and a horizontal line, also halfway down.

Draw the eyes on the center line, add in two additional horizontal guidelines, indicating where the bottom of the nose sits, and where the mouth is.

Erase the guidlines and redefine.

Add in the hair, building it up dimensionlly.

The head from different angles.

THE EYES

The eyes are the most expressive part of the face, and can be drawn in an endless number of ways. Use the eyes to illustrate the personality of your characters.

THE NOSE

The nose on most manga characters, as fans of the genre know, is very small, even tiny. Below are different ways to draw a manga nose.

THE EARS

THE MOUTH

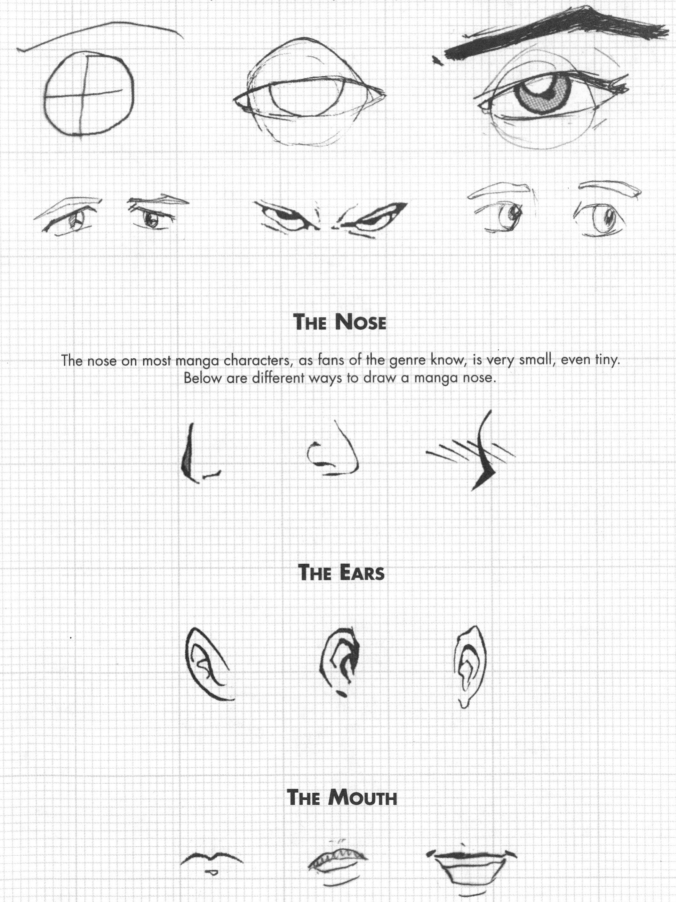

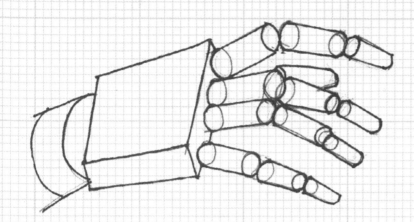

HANDS

When sketching, draw the entire hand, both the foreground and the background. This way the drawing is three-dimensional. Look at your own hands! See how they work mechanically. And remember, don't get discouraged! Every artist has a hard time drawing hands.

When beginning a sketch, draw the hand in geometrical forms first.

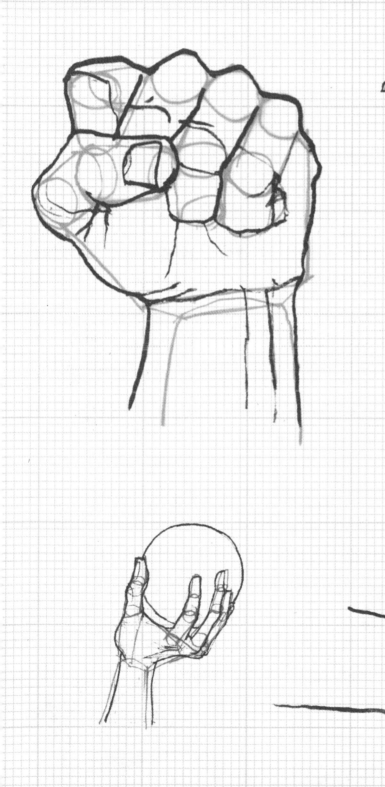

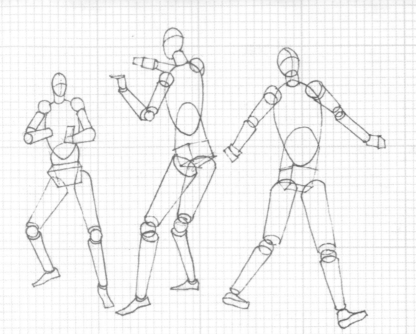

BODY PROPORTIONS

No matter how cool a character or pose is, it has to be built with a solid structure. Keep it simple! Break down the body into simple, easy to draw shapes, using elliptical shapes for the upper body mass and cylinders and balls for the joints and limbs.

The manga figure is generally 8.5 to 9 heads high.

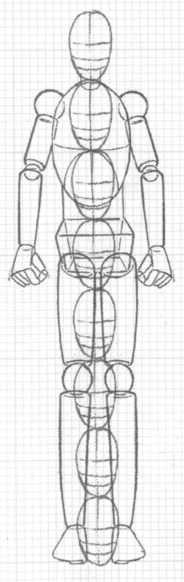

Develop a character scale guide.
Remember to keep your characters at a consistent scale to each other.

GREAT! NOW THAT YOU'VE GOT THE BASICS DOWN, LET'S GET BACK TO BUSINESS!

THE PRETTY BOY

The pretty boy is manga's knight in shining armor. With a devilish grin and windswept hair, he is slender and handsome. He is also generally the leader of his crew, as well as the romantic interest of most stories.

THE UNDERDOG

The underdog is the kid from the wrong side of the tracks who's made good. Small in stature but large in spirit, he is a loyal ally, and can always be counted on in times of crisis.

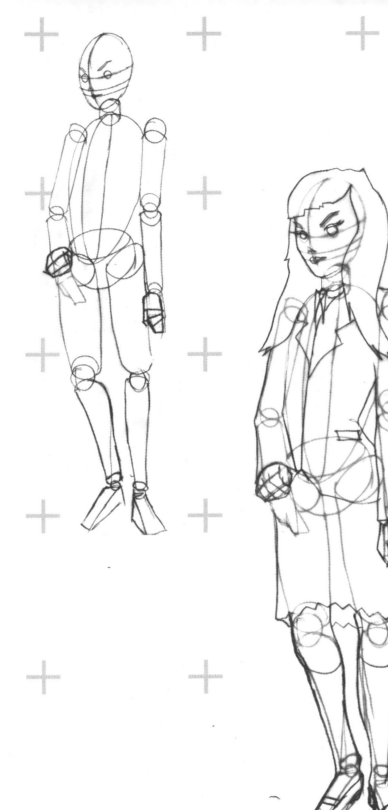

THE SCHOOLGIRL

The schoolgirl is pretty—and also a little vain and pampered. She is highly educated (and not afraid to let everyone know). Although she is often at odds with other female characters, her confidence and intelligence are assets.

There are some basic differences between drawing male and female characters. When drawing a girl make the jaw more tapered and the eyes larger. The iris and pupil should appear shiny and take up more area.

Also, emphasize the eyelashes and upper eyelids, and don't forget to take time drawing the hair! It's very important to the female manga characters. Be creative and try drawing bangs, buns, or sections of hair draping in front of or behind the ears.

VAMP

Unabashed of her feminine wiles, the vamp uses her sensuality to gain the upper hand when confronting enemies.

TOMBOY

The tomboy is a somewhat introverted character who is usually a loner. She is creative and observant, however, and isn't afraid to use a little elbow grease to get the job done.

THAT WAS
COOL!

DON'T KNOW HIS NAME. BUT IF YOU RUN ACROSS HIM IN A DARK ALLEY... JUST RUN.

THE GANGSTER

The gangster is the kingpin of the underworld. Sly and deceptive, he is a master manipulator of both people and situations.

MAN, LOOK AT THIS ONE!

THE WITCH

The witch is a master of wicca and not entirely human. Her knowledge of ancient mysticism makes her a frightening foe.

THE HACKER

The hacker is the technowizard of the underworld. He uses his wealth of obscure mathematical and technical knowledge to crack unbreakable codes and security systems.

ELDER WIZARD

The elder wizard is the old wise man of manga. Seemingly prophetic and unerringly observant, his arcane knowledge and advice is often sought out by adventurers and authority figures alike. The depth of his powers are infinite.

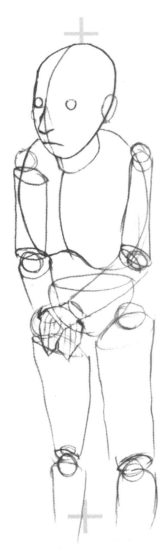

WOMAN SEER

The woman seer or soothsayer is a gypsy-like being, roaming around from one place to another. Often confounding and rarely straightforward, her motherly advice nonetheless puts characters at ease.

CHILD PRODIGY

The child prodigy is the savant of the sages. Her innocence and charms are offset by her intuitive knowledge and vast potential. She is apprentice to the elder sage.

CHAPTER 2: DRAWING MASCOTS, ANIMALS, & MONSTERS

WHERE ARE WE?

LET ME FIND THE LIGHT.

CLICK.

MASCOTS?!?

MASCOTS

Mascots lend mercurial aid and cherubic comedic relief to many a manga plot.

Leoki

Hogachu

Beakle

Puppy McSnuffen

Chi chi-mon

De-monku

HOUSE CATS

Mirthful and mischievous, the house cat is a fearsome predator in it's own mind.

IN THE MANGA UNIVERSE ANIMALS ARE BOTH CUTE AND MONSTROUS, FRIENDLY AND FEROCIOUS, DOMESTICATED AND FERAL. YOU WILL OFTEN FIND THEM BOTH AS KEY PLAYERS AND IN QUIET SUPPORTING ROLES IN YOUR FAVORITE COMIC BOOK.

DOGS

A dog is man's faithful servant and obedient companion.

HORSES

A majestic and powerful beast, the horse is perhaps the most beautiful of all animals.

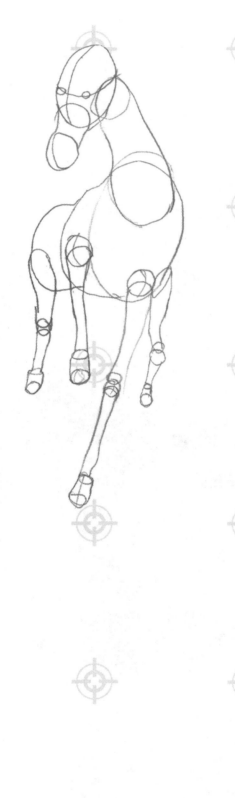

MONKEYS

Man's closest animal relative—clever and playful monkeys are the court jesters of the animal kingdom.

RODENTS

Pest or pet? Both actually. Rodents can at times be somewhat of a nuisance, but their antics can often provide comic relief.

INSECTS

These industrious microinhabitants are the architects of vast miniature societies. Unfortunately for them, these societies rest on the lower rungs of nature's food pyramid.

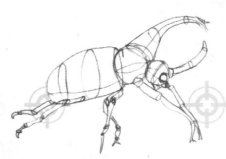

Hornix Beatoxus

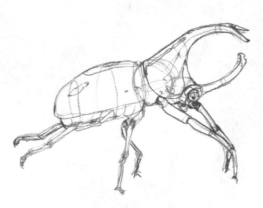

Laborus Anticus

Arachnox

LIZARDS

The modern-day descendent of dinosaurs, these cold-blooded creatures inhabit the hottest deserts and murkiest jungles.

DRAGON

A most ancient evil, the dragon is a staple of folklore and fantasy. Unendingly greedy and elusively wise, he is a menace to towns-people and heroes alike.

GIGASQUID

A hellion from the deep, sailors and ships often fall prey to his tentacled fury.

VAMPIRE

A prince of darkness, the vampire feeds upon the blood of the innocent.

ZOMBIE

Resurrected from the dead, the zombie is driven by the basest of instincts—the appetite for flesh.

WEREWOLF

Part man, part wolf, the werewolf's feral power is intertwined with the lunar cycle.

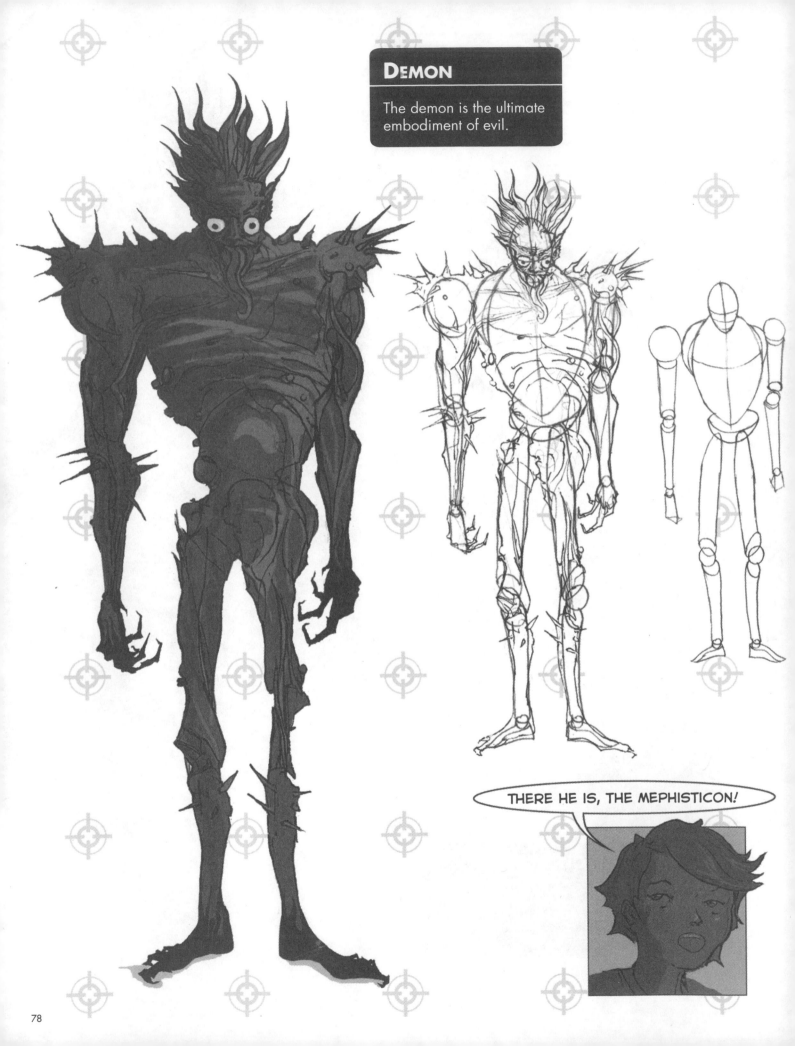

DEMON

The demon is the ultimate embodiment of evil.

THERE HE IS, THE MEPHISTICON!

JUST LIKE THE SAGES SAID.
MAN, IS HE UGLY. ARE YOU SURE YOU'RE READY TO DO THIS?
NO. BUT WE HAVE TO IF WANT TO FIND OUT WHERE MOXIE IS.
COME ON, RELEASE HIM.
MEPHISTICON
RELEASE
JUST ONE MORE BUTTON TO PUSH.
KRACK
UH OH,
I HAVE A BAD FEELING ABOUT THIS.

CHAPTER 3: DRAWING MECHA & TECHNOLOGY

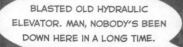

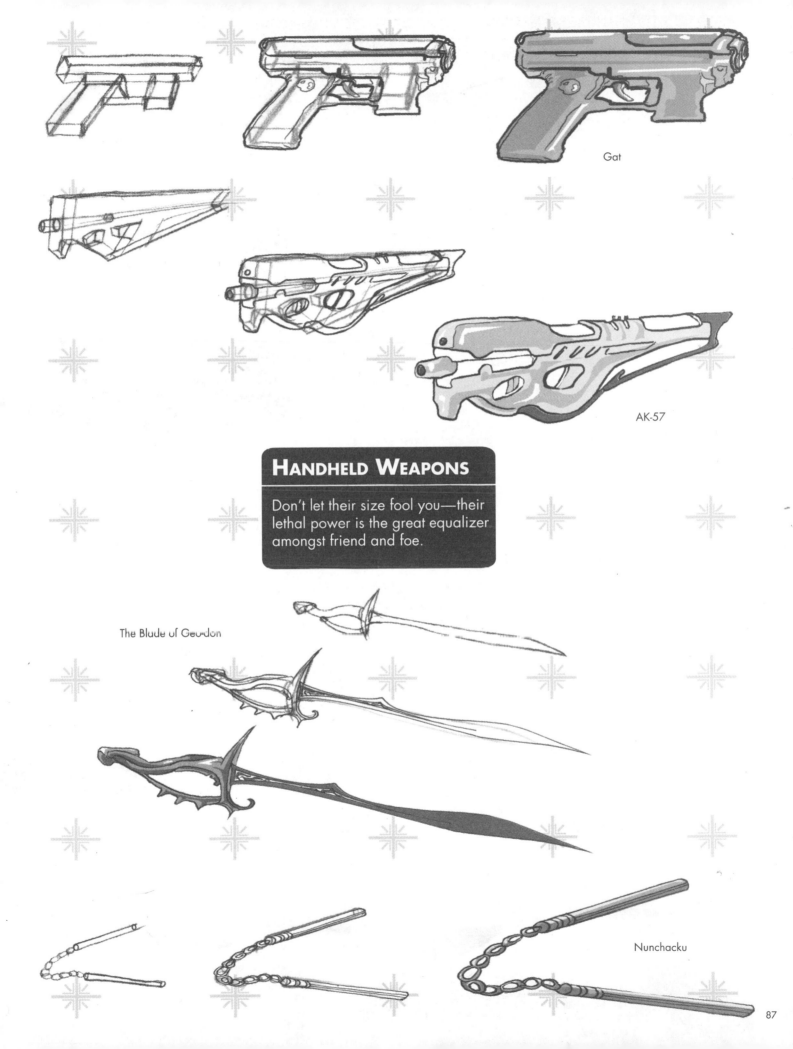

Gat

AK-57

HANDHELD WEAPONS

Don't let their size fool you—their lethal power is the great equalizer amongst friend and foe.

The Blade of Geudon

Nunchacku

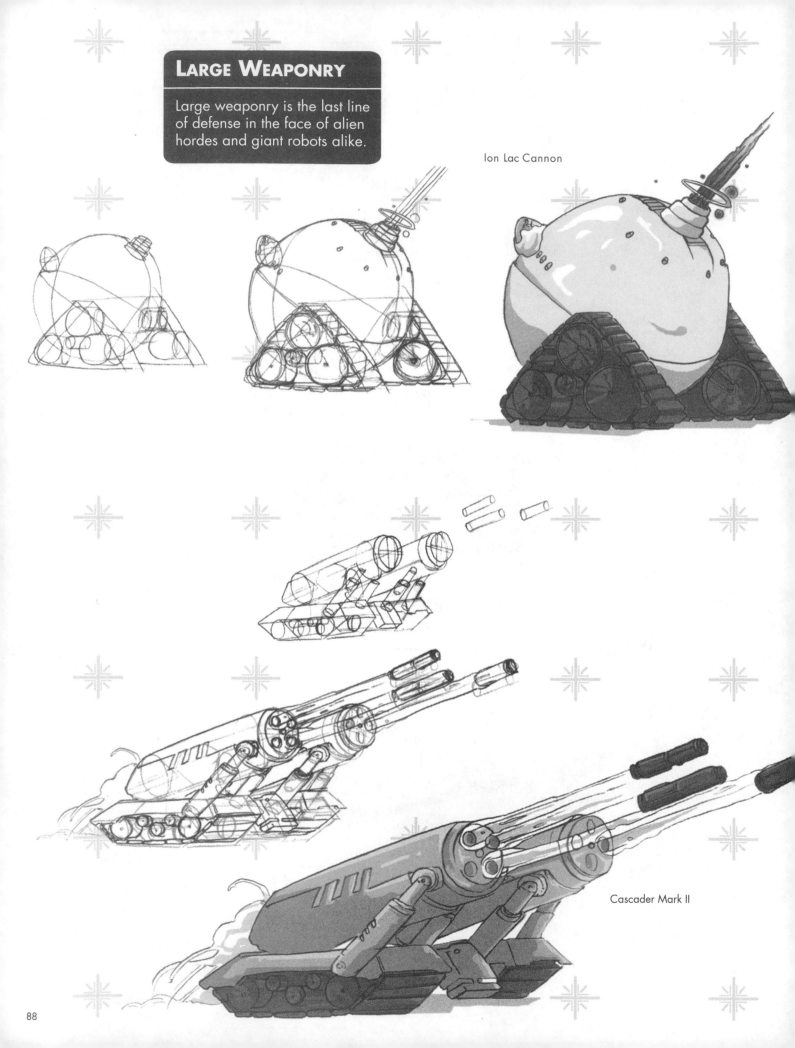

LARGE WEAPONRY

Large weaponry is the last line of defense in the face of alien hordes and giant robots alike.

Ion Lac Cannon

Cascader Mark II

RADAR DISH

A preemptive defense mechanism, little escapes this tireless sentinel.

SATELLITE

The satellite is the hub of interstellar communications, orbiting planets and relaying messages to and fro.

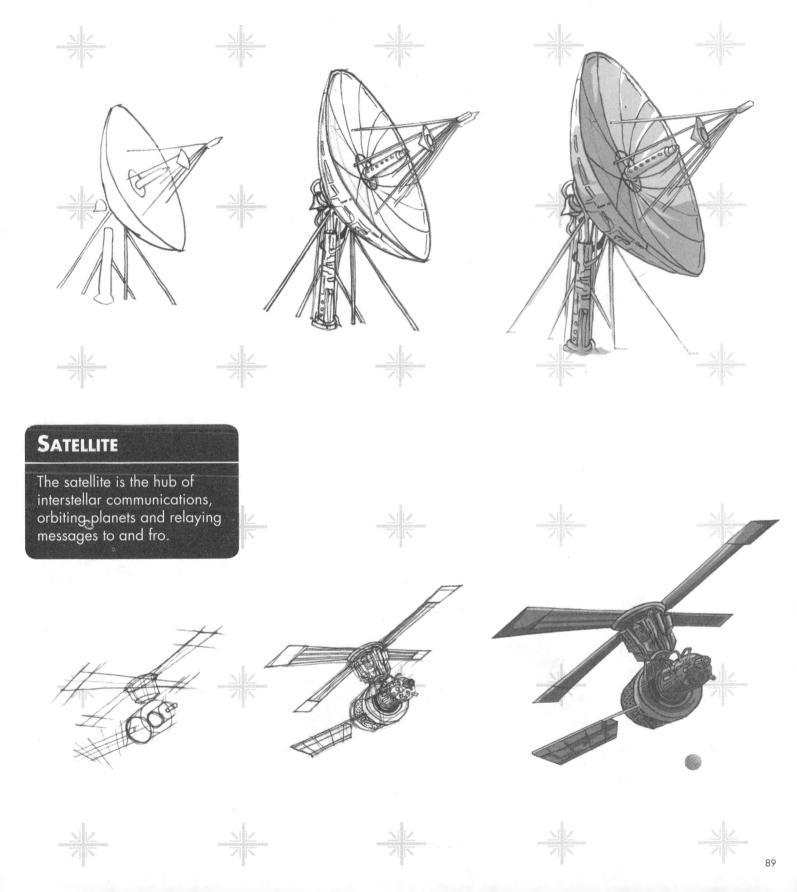

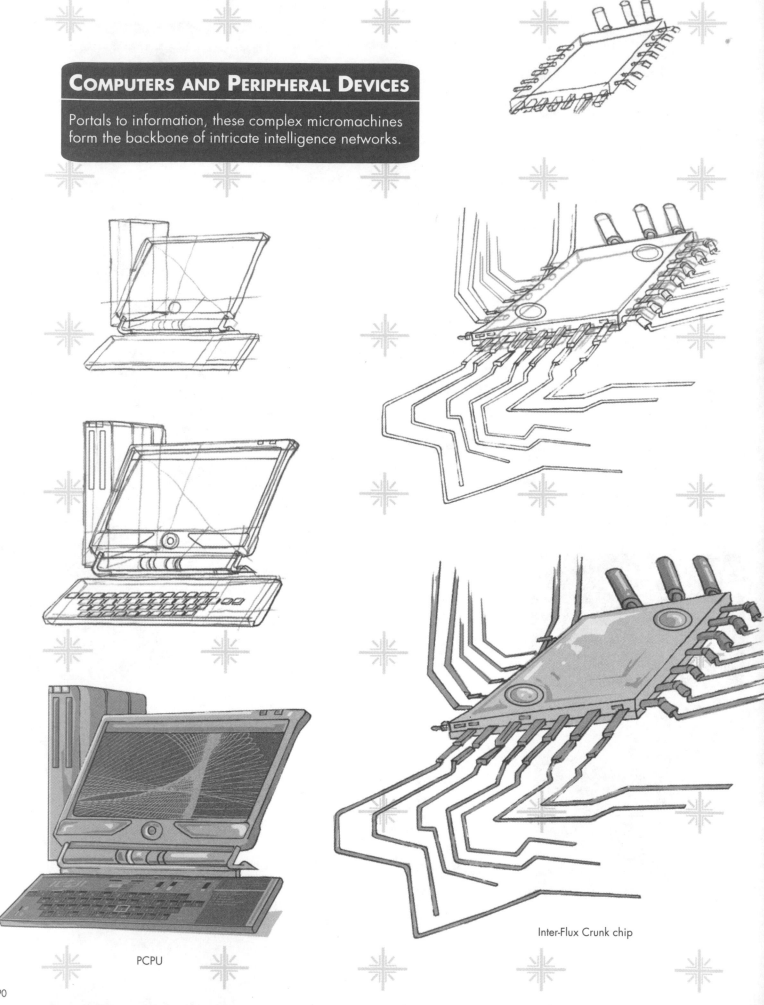

COMPUTERS AND PERIPHERAL DEVICES

Portals to information, these complex micromachines form the backbone of intricate intelligence networks.

PCPU

Inter-Flux Crunk chip

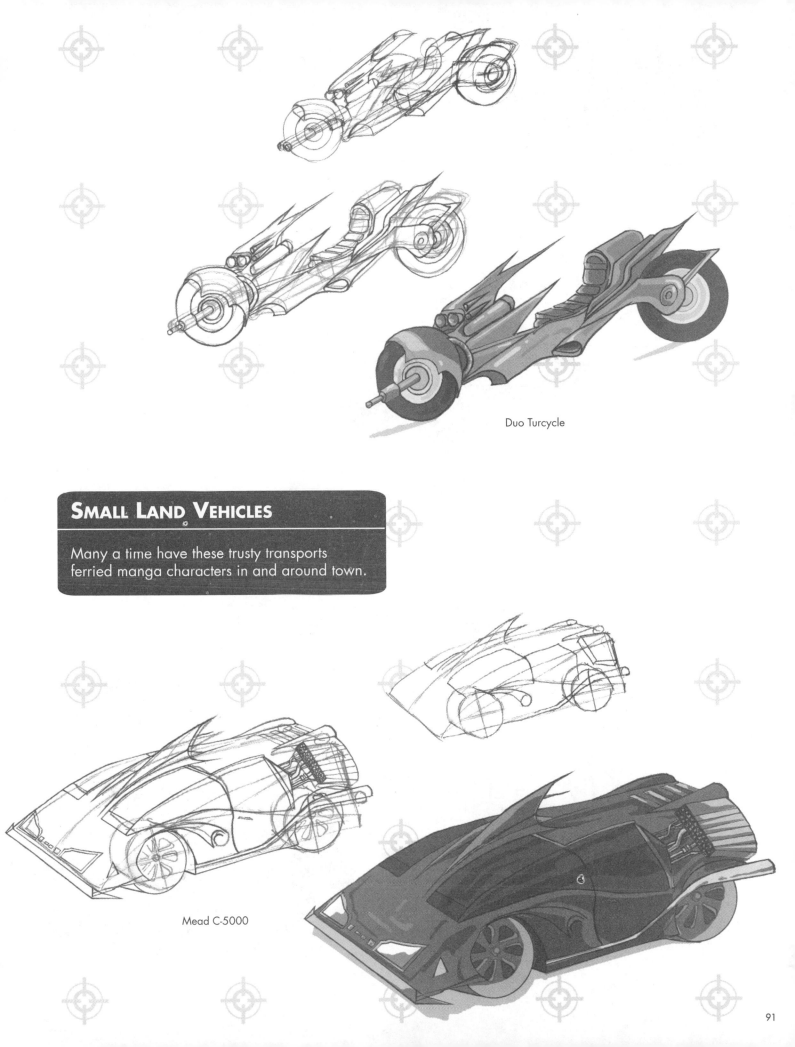

Duo Turcycle

SMALL LAND VEHICLES

Many a time have these trusty transports ferried manga characters in and around town.

Mead C-5000

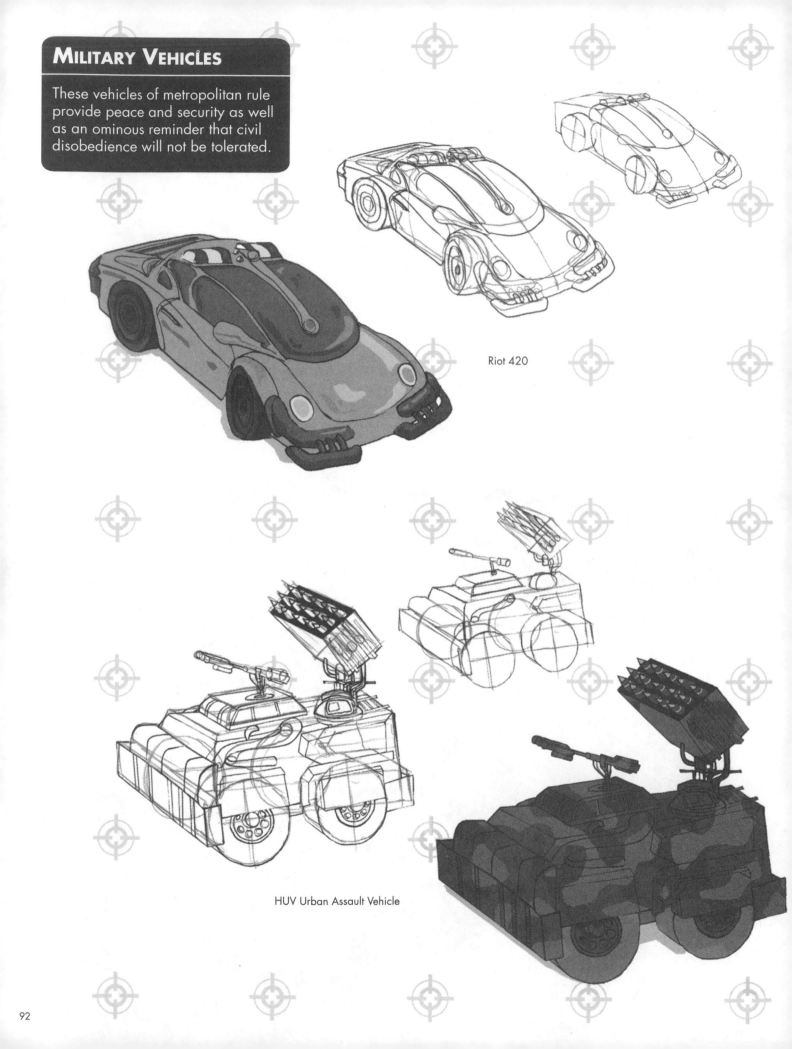

MILITARY VEHICLES

These vehicles of metropolitan rule provide peace and security as well as an ominous reminder that civil disobedience will not be tolerated.

Riot 420

HUV Urban Assault Vehicle

G-Trix Missile Launcher

Heavy Armored Transport

AERIAL ASSAULT VEHICLES

The first wave in a successful attack, these aerial predators strike fear in the hearts of those who oppose them.

Erhund XIII

H Fighter

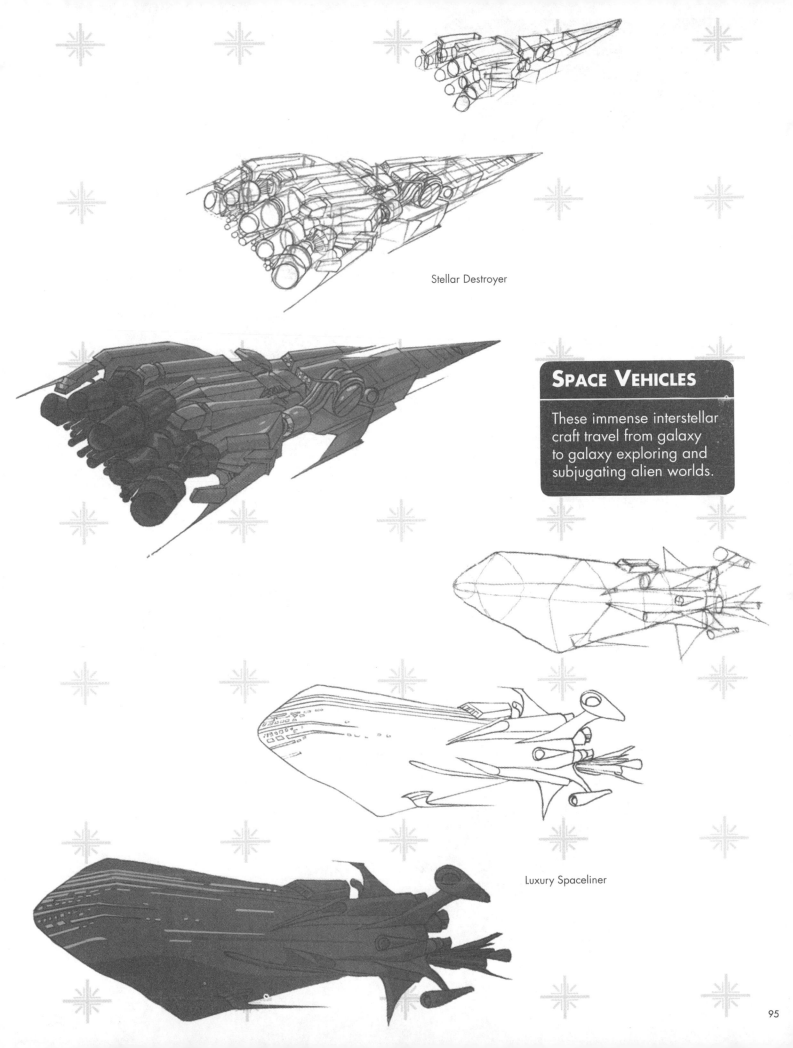

Stellar Destroyer

SPACE VEHICLES

These immense interstellar craft travel from galaxy to galaxy exploring and subjugating alien worlds.

Luxury Spaceliner

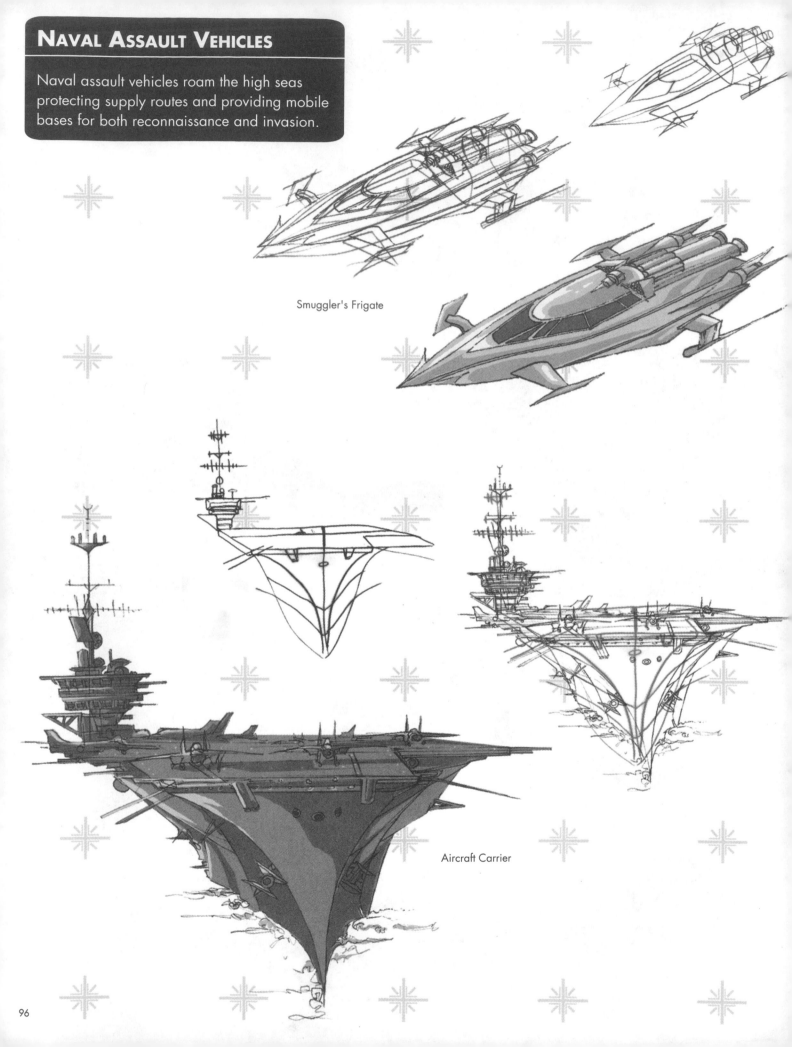

NAVAL ASSAULT VEHICLES

Naval assault vehicles roam the high seas protecting supply routes and providing mobile bases for both reconnaissance and invasion.

Smuggler's Frigate

Aircraft Carrier

MALE MECHA

This battle-hardened robot sees a lot of action on the frontlines, and it shows. His great strength and endurance are an integral part of mecha armies.

AND NOW WE COME TO MY FAVORITE PART OF THE TOUR —THE ROBOTS!

The female mecha is more nimble and agile than her male counterpart.

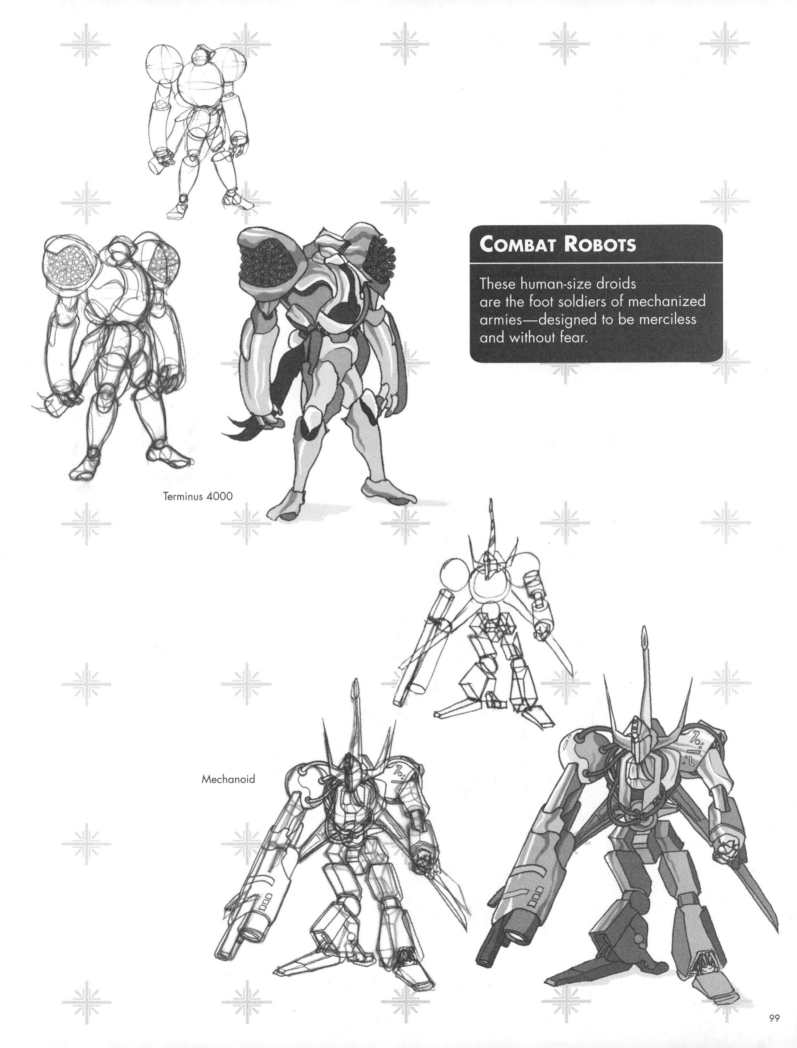

COMBAT ROBOTS

These human-size droids are the foot soldiers of mechanized armies—designed to be merciless and without fear.

Terminus 4000

Mechanoid

LARGE COMBAT ROBOTS

These colossal robots possess unparalleled power and have unlimited destructive capability. Deus ex machina.

Isis XVII

Raidander Go!

These adaptable machines are an invaluable resource in off-world colonization and urban warfare.

VFP (Variable Fighter Plane)

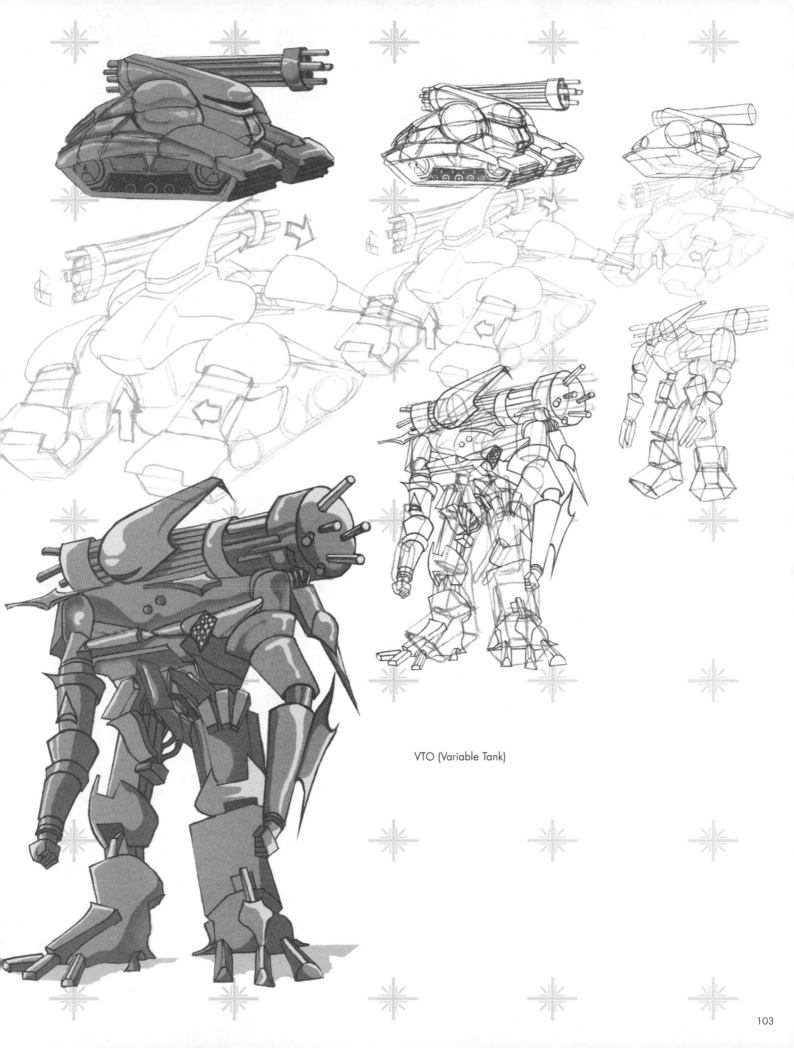

VTO (Variable Tank)

I THINK WE FORGOT ABOUT THE SPEEDER IN THE GARAGE.
THE MONSTERS MUST HAVE SEEN IT AND FIGURED OUT THAT WE WERE IN HERE.

HERE'S YOUR ESCAPE VEHICLE.

WE PICKED UP ON THEIR SCENT, MASTER.

GET IN. I'LL OPEN THE HANGAR DOORS.

VROOOOMMM